To Dear Brian,
A marvello[illegible]
a book is a mirror of th[illegible]
with w[illegible]

5760

29-12-98

(MICHAEL MILSTON)

A CRITICAL REVIEW

Michael Milston

MINERVA PRESS
LONDON
MONTREUX LOS ANGELES SYDNEY

A CRITICAL REVIEW

ISBN 1 86106 3415

First Published 1997 by
MINERVA PRESS
195 Knightsbridge
London SW7 1RE

Printed in Great Britain for Minerva Press

A CRITICAL REVIEW

DEDICATED TO MY FATHER
IVOR MILSTON

Who read the first review and who would have loved to have read all the others.

May his revered name be remembered for a blessing.

About the Author

The author divides his time between reviewing books, teaching English as a foreign language and teaching students who are dyslexic.

In obtaining a BA Degree in Philosophy at the University of London, the author specialised in Philosophy of Religion which included a dissertation on 'Theories of Evil'. The author is a founder-member of *Daled Av*, an organisation dedicated to having a fast-day to commemorate the Holocaust and has had several papers published on the subject. He has also had papers published on the link between left-handedness and dyslexia.

He is, at present, preparing three new papers for publication. The first involves the link between Wittgenstenian linguistics and feminism, the second involves the link between Chomsky and the teaching of grammar and the third paper, which is being revised, is on the subject of reassembling the Sanhedrin.

The author has been reviewing books on Jewish philosophy since 1989 for the magazine *Jewish Books News and Reviews*, the products of which are presented in this book. He has studied at Sokachov Yeshiva in Bait Vegan, and in Jerusalem specialising in Daph Hayomi, the learning of one double-sided page of Talmud per day.

Acknowledgements

To Steven Schonberg, Features Editor of *Jewish Books, News and Reviews*
Without whom this book could never have been written as it was he who gave me the books to review.

To Joseph Lavin
Whose spiritual insight and creativity inspired the cover-design of the book.

To Helen Moss
Whose excellent typed manuscripts facilitated the publishing of the book.

To Joan Lipkin-Edwards
Whose resourceful office-agency was always at my disposal when I needed it.

To Coopers & Lybrand, Executors of the Marks Stein Trust
Whose financial help enabled the book to be published.

To Herschie Schneck and James Upton
Whose wisdom I quoted in my reviews.

To the Almighty
For His inspiration and the gifts He gave me.

Permission to reprint articles from *Jewish Books and News Reviews*.

Preface

If one has to pinpoint the most important aspect of book-reviewing it would be the sublimation of the ego of the reviewer to the book. If the book becomes the centre of the review, rather than the critic's opinion of what the book is discussing, then the reader of the review is more likely to want to read the book. The point of a review is that the book itself should cause a reaction in the reader, rather than the reviewer of the book causing a reaction in the reader.

This is not to say that the views of the reviewer cannot become apparent to the reader of the review. By selecting items with which he agrees or which he feels are very profound, he can influence the reader of his reviews. One example of this can be found in my review of Oliver Leaman's *Evil and Suffering in Jewish Philosophy* when I bring to attention the author's idea that one cannot call the Holocaust a punishment because 'it was more likely that less decent people would escape the evil snare of the Nazis because they would be usually more successful in escaping suffering than their more gullible and virtuous peers.' This example contains both an inherent profundity and reflects my agreement.

Use of examples is also very prevalent in my reviews and once more the choice of example is based on originality of thought and concurrence with the opinion of the reviewer. On illustrating the depth of the post-Holocaust philosopher Fackenheim's soul, I took as an example his description of the dancing of Chassidim in Lublin who were 'forced to dance in front of Nazi SS Officer Glowzownik but also changed the Yiddish in their song from "*lamir zich berbetan*" — let us be reconciled — to "*mir welen sei iberleben*" — we shall outlive them. "Glowzownik screamed at the Chassidim to stop but he could not destroy a moment of truth; life does not need to sanctified: it is already holy."' This example both reflects Fackenheim's originality of thought in that the root of the action is holiness and my concurrence with this view.

The ultimate point of a book review is to stimulate ideas and to lead the reader of the review to a clearer concept of life, which in turn leads to a clearer understanding of good and evil, leading ultimately to a better world.

The Book of Theodicy: Translation and Commentary on the Book Of Job

By Sa'adiah Ben Joseph Al-Fayyumi; translated from the Arabic with a philosophic commentary by L. E. Goodman
New Haven; London: Yale University Press, 1988
[ISBN 0 300 03743 0 £55 481p (Yale Judaica series XXV)]

One of the Torah's great strengths is its multifariousness - it encompasses all the great themes of morality. To study Torah is synonymous with the study of morality and depending on where one studies Torah, the relevant theme of morality exists. Nowhere in the Torah, except perhaps the confrontation with Amalek, itself the symbol of absolute evil is the theme of evil so explicit as in the Book of Job.

The Book of Job is about evil and man's reactions to it. L. E. Goodman's exegesis on Sa'adiah Gaon's own exegesis of Job bristles with all the moral issues that the study of evil entails. Goodman's mission in this book is two-fold; firstly to portray the great mind of Sa'adiah Gaon perceiving evil through the Book of Job, and secondly, to show how he perceives evil through Sa'adiah Gaon. It is an exegesis on an exegesis, a mirror on a mirror, or to analogise still further, a training-college which trains teachers to be teacher-trainers.

Goodman is Professor of Philosophy at the University of Hawaii and in his acknowledgements he includes the almost Pythonesque thanks 'to the Chabad Rebbetzen of Honolulu for her careful and cheerful assistance in verifying the Biblical and Midrashic citations'. That such a work should come out of Hawaii is rather like hearing that a Satmar synagogue has opened in Las Vegas, but it really is an excellently researched and balanced book.

Goodman begins with the factual and idealistic background of Sa'adiah Gaon and continually makes the point that Sa'adiah sees Judaism as universal and therefore tries to relate all philosophical concepts to Judaism. For example, Sa'adiah sees the 'Sephir Yetsirah' ascribed to the authorship of Abraham, as dealing with the 'Abrahamic issue', that is the relationship between G–d and his creation. In his commentary Sa'adiah argues against an idea widely held amongst contemporary Jewish teachers, that one should not delve too much into the creation of the world, and mentions that *Gematria* (the use of numbers and letters to comprehend the Holy One) should be used only as a means to that end rather than as an end in itself. Goodman sums up Sa'adiah's philosophy thus: 'The goods of this world are not obstacles but stepping–stones to a higher blessedness which is proved by the very incompleteness of our present gifts to await those who merit it.'

Goodman then turns from discussing Sa'adiah's general philosophy to his philosophy of Job and of evil itself. He discusses both Sa'adiah's interpretation of Job and those of other Jewish and Muslim philosophers. One of the interesting aspects of a philosophical *machloket* is that it is timeless, so that we can have a ninth–century philosopher arguing with one from the twelfth century. One example of this is Sa'adiah's dispute with the exegete Rabbi Isaac Hacohen from the fifteenth century. For Isaac no man can suffer what Job suffered, therefore Job has to be seen on an allegorical level. Sa'adiah will have none of this, proclaiming Job as not only existing but having all of the qualities that exist in the exemplary human–being to reach others, as Goodman puts it, 'to address adversity intellectually as well as morally.' Sa'adiah even ascribes to Job the title of Prophet citing from Avoth de Rabbi Nathan: 'Job prophesied and did not know what he was prophesying ... that Hakodosh Baruch Hu would again give good to him.'

Discussion of evil, therefore, comes from three sources: the Book of Job; Sa'adiah Gaon's exegesis; and Goodman's exegesis on Sa'adiah. Thus, one perceives Goodman's ideas on the interaction of evil with those of both Sa'adiah and of the Book of Job itself. Goodman's view on suffering is that it can transform one from a simple religiosity to 'a complex and intellectual desire to confront and question G–d.' Sa'adiah suggests that G–d's silence on the question of suffering is necessary because if a person knew why he was suffering that itself would dissolve the meaningfulness of that suffering. For Sa'adiah, if one accepts one's lot without knowing the reason one is on a higher *madregah* than if one does not. From the Book of Job itself we have the extraordinary accusation of Satan that Job's faith in G-d is based on the fact that G-d has always been good to him, and it is, therefore, a type of 'cupboard love'. Implicit in this, is the fact that suffering is needed as a test to reveal if one's faith is genuine. There is no discussion here of the Hindu and Jain idea of suffering being caused by one's evil actions in a previous life because this view is not discussed in Job; to enable it to be discussed there would have to be a source from Job in which to base the discussion.

The remaining two-thirds of the book is the translation of the Book of Job by Sa'adiah and his commentary translated from the Arabic by Goodman, with further notes by Goodman himself. This three-way interaction is set out in a three-way arrangement on each page: there is the text of Job itself; Sa'adiah's commentary; and Goodman's notes appearing at the end of each chapter, with each phrase of Sa'adiah that is subject to Goodman's comments being marked with an asterisk. An example of how the three come together can be taken from Job 1:7. This verse is G-d's address to Satan asking him why he is presenting himself with the other angels. Sa'adiah discusses what a question from G-d actually means. He postulates that G-d already knows the answers to the question He is asking. He illustrates this by bringing fifteen other such questions which G-d has asked from Adam to Zechariah. A brilliant example is G-d's question to Amos (Amos 5:3): '"What seest thou, Amos?" and I said "I saw a plum-tree"'. Sa'adiah shows this to be a rhetorical question because G-d obviously knows what Amos is seeing as He is appearing to him at the time. Therefore says Sa'adiah, G-d is only asking Satan the question because 'He has already intended to test Job.' G-d's question 'Whence comest thou?' is put to clear the way for the action to begin — a sort of parliamentary supplementary. Satan's answer 'from roaming this land and travelling through it' is an amended translation by Sa'adiah who interprets '*ba-aretz*' to mean 'this land' rather than 'in the Earth' as it would be meaningless for Satan to say something which he obviously does all the time. On discussing Sa'adiah's observations on the rhetorical question, Goodman introduces the 'heretical' Hiwi-Al-Balithi who argued that these questions were not rhetorical but showed that G-d was not omniscient. Thus, we have Sa'adiah's commentary on Job 1:7 and Goodman's reflections on it adducing even the heretical view of another who interprets the verse differently.

Goodman ends his excellent book with an appendix illustrating various approaches to the translation of the Book of Job. One example that he cites is Sa'adiah's use of the disjunctive (*Ẉaẉ*) making this mean 'or' instead of 'and'. In 6:22 and 6:23, Job says that G-d should either 'consummate my torments' (*Wiyaditeni*) *or* yet again (*Uthi 'od*) 'grant me consolation' (*neḥamathi*). The (*Ẉaẉ*) in (*uthi*) must mean 'or' because Job could not possibly ask G-d to perform two opposite actions at the same time.

The effectiveness of Goodman's technique is demonstrated by the fact that following the excellent translation, the index is superbly laid out: there is a section for Tanach; one for Talmudic, Midrashic and Rabbinic sources; one for philosophical sources ranging from Epicurus through Gersonides to Kant; and concluding with religious Islamic sources, particularly with the Zamakhshari which has a large portion on the link between 'ultimate accountability' and the 'meaning of life' based on the Book of Job. There is a section for proper names and a glossary of all Hebrew, Aramaic and Arabic words and phrases. My only criticism is the transliteration of Hebrew using a very complex phonetic pattern which is not recognisable to the average reader.

Of theodicy, the problem of evil, there may never be a solution because if perfection is without evil and we are made in the image of the Perfect Being, how can we fully understand something outside of us? Perhaps if we see evil both as the enemy of men and of G-d, all becomes clearer. After all, is not the Hebrew of the name 'Job' an anagram of 'enemy'?

The Book of Beliefs and Opinions

By Sa'adiah Gaon, translated from the Arabic and Hebrew by Samuel Rosenblatt

New Haven, London: Yale University Press, 1989
[ISBN 0 300 00865 1 £62.95 519p: 0 500 04490 9 - £13.95 (pbk).]

One of the biggest philosophical and religious myths of the modern world is that somehow modern man is better equipped to discuss the 'whats', 'whys', and 'hows' of morality than our ancient counterparts. A book like Sa'adiah Gaon's *The Book of Beliefs And Opinions* is more than enough to explode the myth. Sa'adiah deals with all the problems that confront modern man and which modern man thinks he is very sophisticated in addressing. One example of Sa'adiah's undoubted superiority over our modern pseudo-thinkers is his addressing of the ethical problems of sacrifice. Unlike the Lubavitch theory that states that animals are uplifted by the honour of being chosen to be sacrificed to G–d and therefore do not suffer, and unlike the Progressive theory that sacrifices are cruel and should be abolished, Sa'adiah puts forward the notion that just as human beings are recompensed in the world to come for the pain they feel in this world, so too are animals. As Sa'adiah puts it: 'G–d would of course compensate the beast in accordance with the excess of the pain'.

As is generally known, Sa'adiah's masterpiece was written in Arabic and has here been translated by Samuel Rosenblatt and this edition published by Yale University Press follows their recent edition of Sa'adiah's commentary on the Book of Job. Unlike Hebrew, which has holy status, Arabic is only chosen by the author so it can be understood by the populace. Rosenblatt's translation has an archaic touch in that he retains the old second and third person singular forms. In explaining a possible refutation of the *ex nihil* proof of creation, Sa'adiah puts into the mouth of the refuter the following: 'How didst thou base thy proof on the premise that there can be no act without an agent rather than the premise that a thing be produced only out of another seeing that these two assertions are of equal force?' Sa'adiah then refutes the refuter by saying that an argument must logically be based on a premise and not on a conclusion. One cannot understand the creative force from the thing that has been created. What is evident in Rosenblatt's translation is both its accuracy and archaism, an extremely effective combination which other modern translators would do well to notice.

Sa'adiah deals with the basis of Judaism under ten different categories beginning with the creation of the world and ending with the golden mean, which deals with the way man should conduct himself in everyday life. What is evident throughout is Sa'adiah's vast general knowledge. One is reminded of the Vilna Gaon's brilliant analogy comparing general knowledge to gift-wrapping paper: one only gets the wrapping if one buys the present, and the Torah is the gift and general knowledge is the wrapping. In his treatise on the Creation, Sa'adiah makes the point that the heavens are just as finite as the earth because we have conception of the heavens. By 'heavens' Sa'adiah alludes to the celestial universe and as it is therefore possible or potentially possible to understand the universe fully, the universe must be finite. It is also impossible, says Sa'adiah, 'for an infinite force to reside in a finite body.' So, therefore, the force of gravity which maintains the universe must be finite with a beginning and an end. It is only the Holy One who has no beginning and therefore anything finite could not be responsible for what happened before *that* beginning.

What is apparent in all Sa'adiah's arguments is their logical presentation. In a brilliant refutation of utilitarianism, which Sa'adiah defines as 'that which causes pain and worry and grief being wrong and that which affords pleasure and rest being right,' Sa'adiah asks what happens when adultery, one of the worst three sins in Judaism, is committed? The pleasure that the adulterer takes occurs exactly at the same time as the pain of the wronged partner. 'Any theory' says Sa'adiah, 'that leads to such internal contradiction and mutual exclusion must be false'.

Finally, what separates Sa'adiah from most of the philosophers, including from Spinoza to Schopenhauer, is his use of scripture to vindicate his statements. For Sa'adiah, the Torah is G–d's guide on behaviour between man and G–d '*ben adam umakom*' and man and man '*ben adam uḥavero*'. He tries to imagine what the world would look like without Torah and makes the interesting but debatable assertion that one result would be that stealing would become impossible because everything would be stolen and one cannot steal from a thief! It is interesting that a thousand years later, during the Holocaust, Rabbi Oshri ruled in a responsum that it was permissible for Jews in the Kovno ghetto to steal wood from the 'accursed Germans' to build a *Succah* because they themselves had stolen the wood from Lithuanian Jewish timber-merchants. Such is an example of the timelessness of Sa'adiah's wisdom. It is therefore delightful to find Sa'adiah, at the end of each of his logical proofs, quoting a scriptural source in vindication. Not only does he quote the verse but he gives greater weight to that than to his logical proof. In refuting the heretical view that it is inconceivable that G-d would abandon his angels in favour of earthly life-forms thus questioning the whole of the creative process, Sa'adiah asks how do we know that G-d abandoned his angels? It is just as possible that G-d 'could have caused many times as much light to dwell in their midst as He had put among men' but says Sa'adiah 'there is *no need* to bring up this argument in view of the fact that scripture says: G-d is to be proclaimed by the great council of the Holy Ones and to be feared in reverence of all them that are about him (Psalm 89, v.8).' It is said that when Shimon ben Jochai went to heaven G-d himself rose up to greet him; perhaps when Sa'adiah went to heaven, G-d invited him to sit at the great council of the Holy Ones.

Crisis and Covenant - Jewish Thought After the Holocaust

By Rabbi Jonathan Sacks
Manchester: Manchester University Press, 1992.
[ISBN 0 7190 3300 4 £45.00 294P]

The best adjective to describe this very ambitious book by Rabbi Sacks is 'courageous'. It is courageous firstly because it confronts the Holocaust both intellectually and emotionally. It requires courage to write, as Rabbi Sacks does, of the sickening actions by Franz Stangl, Commandant of Treblinka, who 'insisted that pious Jews be made to spit on Torah scrolls and that when they ran out of spittle more should be supplied by spitting into their mouths.' It is courageous secondly because it seeks to indict the post-Holocaust generation for its failure to come to terms with the enormous catastrophe. In quoting from Rabbi Soloveitchik's great masterpiece, *Kol Dodi Dophek* ('The Voice of My Lover is Knocking') he compares the Holocaust and the result of the Holocaust to Pesach and Shavuoth. For Rabbi Soloveitchik, Pesach epitomises the *Brith Gorel* - the Covenant of Fate - when we are affected by the fate of history and Shavuoth epitomises the *Brith Ye'ud* - the Covenant of Destiny - when we act on the way the fate of history affects us. For Rabbi Sacks we have had our *Brith Gorel* - we have been affected by the fate of the Holocaust but we have not yet enacted the *Brith Ye'ud* - we have not acted on it. 'That', writes Rabbi Sacks 'from the religious perspective, is the tragedy and the challenge'.

Rabbi Sacks seeks to understand World Jewry's reaction to the Holocaust by attempting to chart World Jewry's intellectual evolution up to the Holocaust. In doing this he makes a number of generalisations, not completely accurate, in which he tries to equate events with the Jewish psyche. The French Revolution, for example 'ended the Jew's status as an outsider' and, therefore, after that Jews took a more prominent role in public affairs. However, there were Jews like Maimonides, Nachmanides, Abarbanel and the Maharal who took extremely prominent roles in their respective societies. However, what must be said is that Rabbi Sacks' great strength throughout this intellectual evolutionary chart is not only his grasp of other people's ideas, but his ability to articulate them. In discussing the Zionistic philosophy of Moses Hess he pinpoints the birth of secular Zionism as the means to extricate World Jewry from the frying pan of assimilation to the fire of anti-Semitism. In summing up the philosophy of Rabbi Abraham Isaac Kook's religious Zionism, he shows Kook's equation with returning to Eretz Yisrael and the beginning of the Messianic Era and how Kook foresaw the terrible events that would occur outside Eretz Yisrael culminating 'in the birthpangs of the Messianic Age'.

Sacks also allows a sense of humour to infringe on his analysis on certain unsavoury philosophies on Jews and Judaism. He quotes a tirade by Voltaire on the Jewish people, which makes M. Le Pen sound almost reasonable, and ends the quote by adding *'in a generous afterthought,* Voltaire added, still we ought not to burn them'.

But it is in his role in discussing how Jewish ideas have been shaped since the Holocaust that Rabbi Sacks really shines. Rabbi Sacks basically divides post-Holocaust thought into those who think that the Holocaust is unique and those who do not think it is unique. Sacks then introduces the Latin word '*novum*', first coined by the philosopher Fackenheim, as an umbrella-word for all those who regard the Holocaust as unique. For Fackenheim, himself, because the Holocaust is unique then Post-Holocaust Judaism has to incorporate it, both in its philosophy and observation. Fackenheim makes the fascinating and controversial idea that even total Secularists have been made more religious by the Holocaust: 'the Secularist Jew believes more because post-Holocaust Jewish survival is itself a testimony of faith'.

One aspect of *Novum*-thought in the Holocaust that Rabbi Sacks neglects to mention is the Amalek theory. Amalek may be best defined as the three-dimensional reflection of evil as first perceived through the Amalkites in Exodus. The Torah commands us to both remember and eradicate Amalek. If the Holocaust were perpetrated by Amalek, if Auschwitz is the epitome of Amalek on Earth, then Judaism has to reflect it in its philosophy and observations. It would, for example, perceive the destruction of the First and Second Temples as a punishment but would perceive the destruction of one-third of our people as a result of not remembering Amalek, which in the case of the Holocaust was even more evil than a punishment. Irvine Greenberg offers the *novum*-orientated notion that because of the Holocaust, Judaism is entering a third epoch. The first epoch until the destruction of the Temples is exemplified by Torah *Shel Bichtov* (the written Torah) and the second epoch because of the dispersion of Jewry is exemplified by Torah *Shel B'ael Peh* (Rabbinic Judaism). Greenberg sees the second development as the Face of G-d being made less prominent by Rabbinic injunction. He sees the post-Holocaust epoch as the Face of G-d being made even less prominent as, according to Greenberg, it is impossible to understand G-d in the light of the first two developments. In the third epoch, institutional Judaism will prevail with G-d being seen in these institutions. Sacks sums up 'the key to this configuration is an emphasis on human initiative on taking the Jewish destiny into one's hands'. But perhaps the most intriguing and without doubt the most mystical novum-orientated thinker was Rabbi Kalanymos Shapiro, murdered in the Warsaw Ghetto in 1943. 'As a result of the Holocaust', he preached to our impoverished brothers, 'we must cry with G-d'. Shapiro explained that we must enter into how G-d is feeling as He witnesses His people, Israel reduced to the state that they found themselves. Man must cry with G-d and enter into his 'secret chamber of weeping.' Rabbi Kalanymos asks, 'Why is there a secret chamber?' 'Because if there were a single tear of Divine weeping to enter into the world, evil would no longer exist'. The tear would consume the world and all those in it and G-d's promise to Noah would be broken; hence G-d had to have a secret chamber. Elie Wiesel echoed this in his book *Night* when on witnessing a boy of three being hung by the Germans, he declared 'G-d himself is crying on this day'.

The non-*novum* orientated thinkers cited by Rabbi Sacks include the Satmar Rebbe who saw the Holocaust, as he saw the destruction of the Two Temples, as a punishment, but this time because of an attempt to politicise the coming of the Messiah. Rabbi Sacks omits, however, the conclusion to his remarks that had this politicisation ceased after the Holocaust, the Holocaust itself would have been the birthpangs of Moshiach, the defeat of Germany would have been the defeat of Gog and Magog and that this would therefore have heralded the coming of Moshiach. Of course, it is possible to be a religious Zionist and have the same view as the Satmar Rebbe of the link between the Holocaust and the coming of Moshiach but in the case of the religious Zionist there is no reason why the Moshiach should not come now as he would see nothing wrong in a state as a prelude to Moshiach. Eliezar Berkovitz sees the Holocaust as the means by which the Jewish people reached their highest spiritual point. He gives an amazing insight into the spirituality of our brethren in the Holocaust: 'If at the moment before death he is able to accept his radical abandonment by G–d as a gift from G–d then he has achieved the highest form of *Kiddush Hashem*'.

Rabbi Elchanan Wasserman, murdered by the Nazis in Lithuania in 1941, saw the Holocaust as a *Churban* (sacrifice). In a speech to his Yeshiva students before he and they were taken to be murdered by the Germans, he proclaimed that Jews were being sacrificed for the restoration of the Jewish people. Therefore, as the Jew goes to his death he must have no impure thoughts as an 'improper thought would make the sacrifice *Pigul* [invalidated]'.

But perhaps the most thought-provoking thinker of all is one who combined both *novum* and non-*novum* thought in evaluating the Holocaust. For Michael Wyschogrod the *Novum* of the Holocaust is to push us *back* to the Non-*Novum* of original Jewish thought. The basic premise of Judaism, says Wyschogrod, is that Jews are chosen to emanate world values. G–d did not choose to reveal the truth from those 'who have faith or who obey G–d's Commandments but chose the seed of Abraham, Isaac and Jacob'. The Jewish body as well as the Jewish soul is holy. The Holocaust, in seeking to destroy the Jewish body, reminds us of the holiness of the Jewish body. The fact that the Germans chose us for genocide reminds us that G–d chose us for morality. The evil of the Holocaust is therefore the total negation of the good of G–d.

Rabbi Sacks has, with intellectual erudition, brought us to the point where we await Rabbi Soloveitchik's *Brith Ye'ud*, where we await World Jewry to act in a unified voice, where we await the Atzereth to the liberation of Auschwitz. Maybe this brilliant and courageous book will be the catalyst which makes this come about.

Essays on Judaism, Human Values and the Jewish State

By Yeshayahu Leibowitz, Edited by Eliezar Goldman
Cambridge - Massachusetts
London: Harvard University Press, 1992
[ISBN 0 6 14 48755 3 £31.95 291p]

The point that needs to be emphasised again and again in reviewing any work of Leibowitz is that he is a deeply religious man who argues from a Judaic point of view on any topic whether it be political, philosophical or sociological. The editor of this fascinating collection of essays brings one particular essay, written in 1980, in which Leibowitz quotes from Ezekiel to condemn the stand, as he sees it, of those who believe in the creation of undivided Eretz Yisrael *now*. Ezekiel postulates that when one man - Abraham - inherited the land, Torah was kept but when many have inherited the land, Torah is not kept: 'You eat with blood, you lift up your eyes towards idols, you shed blood and you should possess the land? 33:24–25.' Therefore, says Leibowitz 'to speak of the Divine promise to Abraham and his issue as a gratuitous gift but to ignore the conditions of this promise and to disregard the obligation that it confers on the receivers is a degradation and desecration of the religious faith.' The point that has to be made here, is that Leibowitz bases his opposition to an undivided Eretz Yisrael in the present on Judaic sources, unlike the Israeli Left who oppose it for other reasons. The fact that one can base one's argument for keeping Eretz Yisrael on Judaic principles does not mean that one cannot base one's argument against keeping Eretz Yisrael on Judaic principles.

Another point that needs to be made is that we are dealing with a brilliant post-war philosopher on a par with Fackenheim, Herschel and Louis Jacobs. Not only can he be compared to them but often his views coincide with theirs. His view, for example, on the importance of Halacha evolving to meeting new situations, is very close to Louis Jacobs. In an essay written as long ago as 1952, Leibowitz makes the brilliant observation that Halacha developed in the Diaspora and is therefore not equipped in dealing with matters pertaining to the running of a Jewish state: 'Religious thinking must make the transition to the realities of the State of Israel - it cannot do so without introducing innovation into the religious way of life, into the Halacha itself.' Leibowitz makes the amusing observation that Joseph Caro, in the first verse of *Orach Hayim* in the *Shulchan Aruch*, urges the Jew to 'gird up strength like a lion, to rise in the morning and to serve his Creator.' But he could only do that, says Leibowitz, because the Turkish Empire was running all the everyday administration of the state: 'had Caro not been able to take for granted an existing system of law-and-order, he would have had to write a very different *Shulchan Aruch*.' Like many Orthodox Jewish radicals, including Louis Jacobs, the radicalism of Leibowitz's Judaism is contained in Judaism, itself.

This fascinating collection of essays is edited by Eliezar Goldman, himself an embryonic philosopher except that his language is much more complicated than that of Leibowitz. The irony is that along with Messrs. Navon, Jacobson, Levi and Levy, he assisted in the excellent translation of Leibowitz's essays. In discussing the so-called 'theological agnosticism' of Leibowitz, in which as an extension of Maimonedian philosophy G-d's revelation cannot even be demonstrated, Goldman writes, 'criticism of Leibowitz has taken this theological agnosticism for atheism, without realising that it is but a working-out of the implications of a theology which insists on total transcendence of the Divine'.

Goldman also has the annoying habit of ending each of his comments on Leibowitz's essays with the prefix 'Ed' which, as he is the only person commentating, is totally superfluous. 'Ed' tends also to reveal his own views on whatever Leibowitz is discussing as, for example, on Leibowitz's views on separating religion from state when he quotes Ben-Gurion's famous dictum 'Israel is a state ruled by law and not by Halachah', which Leibowitz as a total Halachist completely repudiates. Thus Leibowitz's basic premise is that every action a Jew makes must be based on Halacha and be an end in itself because if it is a means to an end then Judaism is devalued. The vein which runs throughout his philosophy is that Judaism must in no way be compromised or devalued. His views on the total separation of religion from state stem from the fact that he believes Judaism is compromised if it relies upon the secular state: 'There is no greater degradation of religion than maintenance of its institutions by a secular state - nothing restricts its influence or diminishes its persuasiveness more than investing secular functions with a religious aura.' The problem with this idea is that it assumes that a Jew can be secular whereas one could equally argue that a secular Jew is in essence the same as a Jew who sins. If a secular Jew smokes on the Sabbath it is in essence no different to a non-secular Jew smoking on the Sabbath. In that case, one could argue that secular functions need a religious aura to prevent secular Jews becoming even more secular. Leibowitz would counter this, however, by emphasising the positive values of a total separation of the holy and the profane: 'The separation of religion and state... would signify the beginning of the great confrontation between Judaism and secularism within Jewry and the Jewish state and initiate a general struggle between the hearts and minds of our citizens.' Like Tony Benn, he would argue that policy must change from the bottom upwards not from the top downwards. It is in the streets of Israel where the battle must be won not in the Knesseth.

The other way in which Leibowitz feels that Judaism is compromised is in the Israeli administration of Judea and Samaria. For Leibowitz, the essence of colonisation produces the seeds of anti-Judaic action. In order to keep the population of any colony in check one has to initiate actions which *ipso facto* are against Halacha. There will be a situation where there is a state 'dominated by security police where it is unlikely that human rights and civil freedoms can exist.' This in turn will lead to what Leibowitz calls 'counterfeit religion' which 'imputes to the state supreme value from a religious standpoint'. If one accepts Leibowitz's premise, then everything he says may well follow but if one's premise is that Judea and Samaria do indeed belong to the Jewish people, then it is not a colony as a definition of a colony is someone's land ruled by another. One cannot therefore, apply anti-colonial rationality if it is not a colony in the first place. One cannot use the results of one premise to cure a different premise.

One of the most brilliant aspects of Leibowitz's ability to philosophise is his use of analogy to prove a point. In his essay written in 1980, on the status of women in Halachah, (at present topical because of events within one Synagogue in the United Synagogue movement,) he presents a brilliant analogy as to why women are actually being unholy when they wish to do things they are not bound to do. If the Torah as the source of holiness exempts women from doing certain actions and they then commit these actions then they are being *unholy* because they go against the source of holiness. They are like 'Israelites who would voluntarily begin observing prohibitions applying to priests.' Or, to take Leibowitz's brilliant analogy further, one could compare women wishing to have their own *Minyan* to Israelites who wish to *Duchan*, thus taking part in the Priestly Blessing. Leibowitz sums up in his forceful style, 'This would not imply fear of G–d, love of G–d or service of G–d. It would be totally pointless.'

The other very interesting aspect of Leibowitz's philosophy is his ability to spot sociological trends in contemporary society. In discussing modern Israeli society, Leibowitz writes, 'On Muslim holidays all construction work stops. On the same day hundreds of Jewish restaurants close down all over the country, since most of the kitchen staff are Arabs... our society is such that the normalcy of the life of Jews is dependent on the work of Arabs.'

Leibowitz's strength is his ability to argue any point in the most thought–provoking manner. It would be a catastrophe if he were not appreciated as the great thinker he is. Perhaps the moral of this penetrating book is that one does not have to agree with a thinker to appreciate his thought. If this moral be absorbed by all those who read the book then this can only be of benefit to world Jewry as a whole.

Idolatry

By Halbertal and Margalit
Cambridge, Massachusetts, London
Harvard University Press
[ISBN 0 674 44312 8: £31.95, 295P]

The great achievement of this book is not just that it deals with a subject about which not a lot has been written but that it deals with it profoundly, in a very readable manner. Its ethos is not only to deal with the Judaic definition of idolatry but also to analyse differences contained in Judaism itself with regard to idolatry. For example, Gersonides and Crescas differed from Maimonides in the definition of a predicate when applied to G–d. For Gersonides and Crescas the predicate would be part of G–d whereas for Maimonides it added something to G–d. This is why Maimonides opposed literal language when it was applied to G–d. For Maimonides, a linguistic description of G–d was as misleading as a pictorial representation of G–d.

In the introduction to the book the joint authors write that 'we are interested in various models of idolatry in monotheistic religions especially in Judaism' but one must observe that the book is almost entirely based on a Judaic analysis of idolatry with only ephemeral references to other ideas. Hegel, for example, is brought in on the section dealing with Maimonides because he distinguishes between religious and philosophical language when talking about G–d, accepting the latter and not the former, whereas Maimonides did not accept the credibility of any language in talking about G–d.

The authors begin their analysis of idolatry with the way it is viewed from the *Tanach*. They quote from three prophets, namely Jeremiah, Ezekiel and Hosea. All three prophets compare Israel's idolatry to adultery as if to compare Israel's rejection of G–d to a wife's rejection of her husband. Jeremiah quotes from the Halachah concerning the ban of a man remarrying his ex–wife should she go to another man, 'if a man divorces his wife and she leaves him and marries another man can he ever go back to her?... now you [Israel] have whored with so many lovers can you return to me?' (3:1). Ezekiel was even more extreme than Jeremiah claiming Israel's idolatry to be even worse than a whore because at least a whore takes a fee for what she does whereas Israel was prepared to do as she does for no fee at all, 'You are not like a prostitute for you spurned fees... you made gifts to all your lovers and bribed them to come to you from every corner for your harlotries. (16:32–33).' Ezekiel chides Israel for using the very gifts G–d gave Israel for other lovers – 'the food, the oil and the honey which I provided for you to eat – you set before them for a pleasing odour' (16:19). Ezekiel's anger knows no bounds, even the phrase '*watphasqi eth-raglayich*' – 'and you have opened wide your legs' – is used to emphasise the ease with which Israel is seduced towards other cultures. It must be mentioned here that this section from Ezekiel is not recommended reading for Jews who have assimilated to the cultures of others. Hosea finds a way around the Halachic problem posed by Jeremiah concerning G–d's return to the Jewish people, if G–d views idolatry like adultery. Hosea quotes from the Siphrei on Deuteronomy (306): 'For I am G–d and not a man – the Holy One in your midst' (11:9). If the Torah were given to man as a means to returning to perfection then the law cannot apply to One who is perfect as He has no need to return to perfection. The Torah is therefore the path for man to return to his previous state before his fall. This chapter illustrates the authors' excellent research and choice of quoted extracts as it gives the reader a very clear idea of the metaphorical and perhaps literal link between idolatry and adultery.

In the next chapter the authors excel themselves in their ability to explain the three categories of perceiving G–d – two of which can lead to idolatry. They base the naming of these categories on a publication of collected papers by C. S. Pierce entitled, *The Icon, Index and Symbol.* The first category is entitled 'Similarly-based Representations'. These are basically objects which represent the Divine and which, according to Maimonides, in the Mishnah Torah lead conclusively to Avodah Zarah. Maimonides mentions how gradually the representations come to represent the Divine in the minds of the idolaters and what occurs when these people have children: 'Thus the ordinary folk, including the women and children, did not know of anything but the images of wood and stone and the temples that grew from them... the wise men pretended there was no G-d but the stars and constellations... and there was no-one who knew the Rock of Ages.' (Hilchoth Avodoth Chochavim 1:2).

Pierce's second category is termed, 'Metonymic Representations' from the Greek '*metonomazo*' - to call by a new name. These are manifestations of G-d in that the object is associated with G-d rather than with the representation of Him, an example of this would be the Cherubim on the Aron Kodesh. Apologists of the sin of the Worship of the Golden Calf try to explain the sin away by claiming that Israel saw the Golden Calf as a manifestation of G-d, as a representation of this rather than as a substitution of Him. The authors then quote Onkelos, who is not happy with the idea of Divine Manifestation but sees these objects as a means of Divine Revelation. Onkelos cites the protective Cloud over Israel as a direct causal representation rather than a manifestive representation, in that the Cloud had a causal basis for existence. The third category is termed 'Conventional Representations' which is basically linguistic interpretations of G-d and which has provided a major Machloketh in Judaism as to its permissibility. The authors quote *An'im Zemiroth* as a typical example of conventional representation through language. They quote one of the verses in *An'im Zemiroth*, '*Talalei oroth rosho nimla*' - his head is covered with curls of light - and then claim 'imagine if this line were illustrated and G-d was drawn with a head of curly hair.' Halbertal and Margalit go on to explain brilliantly the difference between linguistic representation and pictorial representation 'the blurring of the distinction between the symbol and the thing symbolised does not occur in language because there is no concrete object that can be endowed with the powers of the symbolised thing'. Thus a word is two dimensional whereas an object is three-dimensional. There are, of course, many in the politically correct nineties who attempt to worship the word itself and Wittgenstein, who considered words to be our servant and not our master, brilliantly coined the term 'epistemological idols' when dealing with those who made words into masters. Feminists who prefer to talk to chairs rather than chairmen fit into this category.

Having defined idolatry, Halbertal and Margalit devote the rest of the book to analysing it. Their greatest strength is the use of example to illustrate certain aspects of idolatry. In trying to illustrate the concept that it is possible to have a situation which is more idolatrous in a Jewish environment than in a non-Jewish environment, Halbertal and Margalit use as an example Saul of Tarsus and Mohammed. Since Christianity has as part of its theological roots an attempted corporeality of G-d, it is nearer to idolatrous thinking than Islam whose concept of G-d is purely monotheistic. Therefore, although Saul of Tarsus was Jewish and, indeed, went to a *Yeshiva*, he is further removed from G-d's monotheism than Mohammed. Therefore, say the authors, 'the use of tradition cannot attest to anything except to define how people who regard themselves as belonging to that tradition intend to use that tradition.' The example of Saul of Tarsus and Mohammed, therefore, illustrates how G-d, himself, can be misused, misinterpreted or made to look perverse in say, for example, the hands of the Jews for Jesus.

However, the highlight of the book was the excellent translation by Naomi Goldblum from the original Hebrew. The standard was such that if one did not know differently one would have supposed that the book was written in English. In discussing the influence of Nachmonides on Kabbalistic thought she translates thus... 'one of the central preoccupations of the Kabbalah was the articulation of G-d as a network of attributes known as *Sephiroth* which are linked to one another in a branched arrangement of emanation and influence.'

This is an excellent book in which all aspects of Judaism are reviewed under the umbrella of possible, idolatrous influences. Even the concept of Amalek is included under the classification of typology. Typology is the means of exposing truths of the past, present and future. Concerning future truths the authors brilliantly postulate: 'Gog may be a distortion of Agag (the Amalekite King) ... and therefore we will continue the struggle with Amalek in the eschatological future.' This book should aid us in this struggle.

To Mend the World

By Emil Fackenheim
Bloomington: Indiana University Press, 1994
[ISBN 0 252 32114 x £37.50 358p(hardback): £15.99(pbk)]

This is a monumental book by a Jew possessed of the enormity of an intellect equalled only by his love of the Jewish people, equalled only by the depths of his soul. His intellect may be perceived in his brilliant exposition of the philosopher Franz Rosenzweig's difference between Judaism and Christianity wherein Judaism precedes the Jew, whereas the Christian precedes Christianity. 'At the time of baptism, Christian parents... only hope that their child will be confirmed. At the time of circumcision Jewish parents know that their son will be Barmitzvahed.' His love of the Jewish people is felt as he writes of the spectacle of concentration camp guards drowning a baby in a bucket of water for twenty minutes in front of its mother. 'One characteristic action of the Holocaust world was the most painful possible murder of Jewish babies ... the reader will remember. How could he forget, that testimony of a Polish guard at the Nuremberg trials.' The depth of soul is revealed in his joy when Chasidim in Lublin, forced to dance in front of Nazi SS Officer Glowzownik, changed the Yiddish in their song from '*lamir zich berbetan*' - 'let us be reconciled' to '*mir welen sei iberleben*' - we shall outlive them.' Glowzownik screamed at the Chasidim to stop, Fackenheim writes, 'but he could not destroy a moment of truth... life does not need to be sanctified it is already holy.'

The first factor that one has to understand in this remarkable book is Fackenheim's use of Holocaust language. They base themselves into two categories - symbolic and conceptual. Fackenheim uses symbolic language continually throughout the book, as signposts from which to launch his various arguments. Auschwitz symbolises total evil as epitomised by the Nazis. Even when Fackenheim discusses another concentration camp he puts it under the umbrella of Auschwitz. In discussing President Eisenhower's visit to liberated Ohrduf concentration camp where Eisenhower rebukes a US soldier for giggling - 'Still having trouble hating them?' - Fackenheim prefaces this account 'Allied Soldiers When They Visit Auschwitz.' Another symbol which Fackenheim uses is the German word '*Musselmanner*'. These people, who Primo Levi poignantly describes 'one hesitates to call them living and one hesitates to call their death – death,' were so overwhelmed by the evil of the SS that they lost the power of thought and being. Fackenheim often refers to the silence of the *Musselmanner* as a symbol of the Holocaust. In one devastating statement he says that the *Musselman* 'is the most notable even, if indeed not, the sole, truly original contribution of the Third Reich to civilisation.'

Fackenheim's use of conceptual language is vitally important as he uses it to bring in concepts which in his brilliance he is actually forming. One such word is '*unwelt*'. In the *unwelt* everything is the opposite of what it should be. 'The logic of the *unwelt* is destruction and this is what holds it together.' It is an evil version of Chelm where all laws are based on absolute evil. An example of the *unwelt* is given by philosopher and survivor Jean Amery, 'On threat of punishment no button could be missing on the striped inmate suit but if you lost one at work there was practically no chance of replacing it.' The *unwelt*, as defined by Amery, was that 'a Jew had the sole duty to disappear from the face of the Earth.' The concept of *Novum* which Jonathan Sacks in his masterpiece, Philosophy of the Holocaust, underlines as the epitome of Fackenheim's Holocaust Philosophy, is the concept of the absolute uniqueness of the Holocaust. With fascinating logic, Fackenheim describes resistance to the Holocaust as a *Novum*, if that which it is resisting is a *Novum*: 'Resistance to this *Novum* in history is a *novum* as well' but can only 'be validated by acts of resistance that actually occurred.' It should also be mentioned that Fackenheim uses particular aspects of the Holocaust as milestones of the Holocaust. One example which he continually uses is the cries of children as they are burnt alive in incinerators or thrown alive into pits. The cries of the children together with Auschwitz and the *Musselman* form Fackenheim's Troika of absolute evil.

In his introduction, Fackenheim lists five reasons why the Holocaust is a *Novum*. However, the root of the *Novum* which continually threads itself throughout the book is that the 'crime' of the Jewish people was that of existing at all. What nourished the *Novum* of the Holocaust was that its victims were 'corpses on vacation' and for one-third of our people the vacation came to an end. To the perpetuators of the Holocaust the children of Abraham, Isaac and Jacob were 'vermin with a human face to be destroyed through the invention and practice of all kinds of humiliation and torture, in the hope that the vermin would not only look like vermin but also think of themselves as such.' As the Polish noblewoman, Pelagia Lewinska, put it, 'they wished... to fill us with contempt towards ourselves and our fellows.' For Fackenheim, the Holocaust is unique. Other catastrophes contain some of the ingredients of the Holocaust but not all of them: 'to link Auschwitz with Hiroshima is not to deepen or widen one's concern with humanity and its future. It is to evoke the impart of Auschwitz and Hiroshima alike.'

The key to the *Novum* of the Holocaust is not to be found in the victim but in the perpetrator. By focusing on the victims one is not focusing on the cause of the Holocaust but on its effect. Fackenheim seeks to show the absolute evil present in all perpetrators of the Holocaust: 'The perpetrators of the Holocaust tortured because they were torturers. They placed torture in their service but even more fervently were they its servants.' The absolute evil was from the *Reichsführer* to the concentration camp guard and on to the population itself. 'Germans could only survive if they proved their Aryan innocence.' By proving their Aryan innocence they 'are implicated in the crime crying to heaven in the screams of the children of Auschwitz and in the no less terrible silence of the *Musselmanner*'. Fackenheim quotes from M. K. Dov Shilansky's book on Himmler's visit to Auschwitz, 'he stepped beside the burning-pit and waited for a pair of gloves. Then he put on the gloves, picked up one of the dead bodies off the pile and threw it into the fire calling out, "at last, I have burned a Jew with my own hands".' This, says Fackenheim, destroys the argument of 'the banality of evil' which excuses the perpetrators of the Holocaust because they were 'enmeshed in a dynamic escalating totalitarian system.' Himmler's relish of the moment he burnt one of the six million dead totally exposes the myth of the banality argument. Only those citizens of the Reich 'defying the Führer's law and in so doing risking forfeiting lives are wholly exempt.'

What is to be found in the victim of the Holocaust is the Ultimate. The Ultimate is an additional name of G-d emanating from the Holocaust where G-d is found in the midst of absolute evil. The Chasidim of Buchenwald found the Ultimate when they exchanged four rations of bread for a pair of *Tephillin*. Rabbi Zvi Hersch Meisels writes in similar vein, 'The *mitzvah* of *Tephillin* was so beloved in Auschwitz for it kept broken spirits from losing their complete faith, even for a moment.' The key to the Ultimate is that their faith was based on *no* insight as to why what was happening to them was happening to them. It was based on them rising above the hell of Auschwitz to be with G-d. 'The concepts of nature and will are inadequate... once again we have touched an Ultimate.'

If the Holocaust is a *Novum* in action it must, therefore, be a *Novum* in thought, as one has to reflect the other – as Descartes found by sheer reductionism. It is, therefore, only possible to, think about the Holocaust if one places one's thought in the Holocaust. Just as we imagine we were slaves in Egypt, we have to imagine we were slaves in Auschwitz. If one focuses one's imagination on one particular aspect of the Holocaust one's thought is 'flattened out into a generalized extremity.' The post-Holocaust Jew, 'must place himself with the victims... he must redirect his focus... on to the Nazi assault in its unflattened out uniqueness.' This is the key to the glimpsing of the horrors of the Holocaust. Not only are psychological theories destroyed, philosophical theories are destroyed as well. Heidegger used his own theory of *Dasein* – the ethics of being – to support Hitler. Spinoza's 'man-in-general' as aped by his German-Jewish disciples, who proposed to embrace Christianity provided it become Unitarian, found himself, on the same train to Auschwitz as the Orthodox Jews of Frankfurt. Rosenzweig's concept of the Jewish nation, being a-historical and therefore above history could no longer be the case after the Holocaust. Kant's Categorical Imperative, the ethics of 'ought', had been used by Eichmann to continue destroying Jewish people even when Germany had already lost the war: 'The Eichmanns of the Third Reich involved the Categorical Imperative on behalf of the destruction of human beings and human dignity so total– no remnant would be left.'

There has, therefore, been a philosophical, psychological and emotional rupture and this can only be repaired through the Ultimate. The post-Holocaust *Tikkun* – from the Hebrew root *Tiqqen*; to mend –

only comes about as the post-Holocaust Jew rises above the Holocaust to G-d not because he understands the Holocaust, but because he does not understand the Holocaust. He then perceives the Ultimate just as the Holocaust Jew did: 'Directly then the *Tikkun* of Pelagia Lewinska... and the Buchenwald Chassidim is the basis of a future Jewish *Tikkun.*' But, says Fackenheim, G-d himself helps the Jew to rise above what he does not understand and then he begins to understand. As the Kabbalist, Gershon Scholem puts it, 'The impulse below calls forth an impulse above.'

The *Na a'seh Venishmah* of the *Novum* of the Holocaust must therefore influence the whole Jewish Year cycle. It affects the Jewish Year both in the commemorative days and festivals it has and the ones it does not have. Fackenheim makes the startling claim that Yom Kippur itself has to accommodate to the Holocaust. Mengele's infamous remark on Yom Kippur that, 'he and not G-d would choose what Jews were to live and what Jews were to die meant that Jews on Yom Kippur must return the throne of judgement usurped by Mengele back to G-d.' There must, because of this new *Na a'seh Vanishmah*, be a day to commemorate the Holocaust. On no account can the Holocaust be incorporated into *Tisha B'Av* because that would suggest that the Holocaust was, in some way, a punishment but 'the mourning on a day to commemorate the Holocaust must be for the children, the mothers, the *Musselmanner* - the whole murdered people in its utter innocence.' On Yom Hashoa or its fasting equivalent, *Daled Av*, the Jew rises above the Holocaust to the Ultimate 'so that the accent is on living and not dying.'

The Satmar Rebbe, who with Rabbi Elchanon Wasserman and Rabbi Israel Shapiro of Grodisk declared the Holocaust 'to be the real birthpangs of the Moshiach,' called post-Holocaust Jewry '*Shiburei Hashiburim*' - broken pieces of pieces already broken. Through this brilliant, perceptive, empathetic and honest book the genius of Fackenheim may make all the pieces come together again.

Judaism and the Doctrine of Creation

By Norbert M. Samuelson
Cambridge: Cambridge University Press 1994.
[ISBN 0 521 45214 7 362p]

The most important moral to come out of this unusual and fascinating book will probably stick in the throat of Western, scientific, Berkeley-educated man, and that is that any theory of creation originating from these times is just as likely to be a myth as one originating from Plato's time. As the book's academic and thoughtful author Norbert Samuelson puts it, 'Any theory of creation must be, as it always has been, a myth... it is a mode of thinking as appropriate to the contemporary period as it was to the worlds of the Hebrew Scriptures and the Classical Rabbis.' In other words the truth is just as likely to be found in Ibn Ezra as it is in Stephen Hawking. Indeed, Samuelson goes further and seeks to prove that contemporary thinkers, because of the continual sand-shifting that goes on in modern thinking, impinge themselves less on public consciousness than older thinkers: 'I can speak about thinkers such as Rashi, Nachmanides and Rosenzweig with confidence that their writings will remain relevant for centuries – however the speculation of scientists such as Carl D. Anderson, David Bohm or even Stephen Hawking could lose all relevance in as little as a few decades.' However, Samuelson concedes that 'the findings of contemporary physics help religious people to fulfil their obligation to understand creation by filling in details of the dogma that by no other means would be accessible.' Therefore science is to be used as a contributor to overall knowledge rather than as a moral quantifier.

This book is a celebration of man's curiosity to know of his origins and it is the same curiosity that leads man to explore the universe. The desire to know if there be a possibility of life on one of Saturn's moons is the same desire to know how life started on this world. As is the case of many books on a universal theme, particularly if the authors are exponents of Judaism, the Judaic version takes centre-stage. It is often believed that Judaism offers only a very narrow view on the creation of the world and this book blows away this myth. Gersonides and Rosenzweig, two of Judaism's greatest philosophers, offer deeply profound insights on the Six Days of Creation. For Gersonides, the Six Days is an illusion merely for the benefit of man to understand the creation in stages, 'Since G-d's act of Creation is invariable, creation itself is a unity. However, as what G-d knows in a single act is only knowable to human beings through a conjunction of Multiple Acts'. It must be stressed that this 'illusion' is real in a phenomenal Kantian sense but in its purest noumenal form the Creation was one timeless act. For Franz Rosenzweig, what emerges from the Torah's account of the Creation, is the concept of '*Nichtnichts*' — the negation of negativity. What appears as nothing is in fact G-d's essence 'free from any limitation.' The space over which G-d hovers in the Torah account of the Creation is Rosenzweig's '*Nichtnichts*'. '*Merachepheth*' – the present form of the verb 'to hover' is used in the Torah because the Negation of Nothingness is G-d, in his purest revealed form which is always 'is', because it is above beginning and end. Thus for Rosenzweig, the fact that Merachepheth is in the present form has unparalleled significance. The evolution of '*Nichtnichts*' into a positive form is shown by the difference the Torah makes between the light created on the First Day and the light created on the Fourth Day. The light on the First Day is the command for the negative to become the positive and therefore this light 'judges the yet-to-be-generated individuals of the world to have or to come to have positive value whereas the light on the Fourth Day is positive and has come to have positive value'. Not only, therefore, does Rosenzweig find the origin of '*Nichtnichts*' in the Torah account of Creation, he also finds the next stage of its development there.

Samuelson makes a distinction between the Jewish philosophers and the Jewish commentators: 'The theological commentators have priority over the philosophical commentators' and therefore for a philosopher to be called a Jewish philosopher his views must be substantiated by the Jewish commentators. Samuelson defines an example of a Jewish philosopher as one who would mirror Rashi's view on the link between this world and the World-to-Come by his 'understanding of the correlation between creation and redemption through the mediation of revelation'. It is also interesting that the Jewish philosopher Gersonides and the Jewish commentator Sforno both talk of the timelessness of the Creation, with Sforno echoing Gersonides that 'no time passes between the first and the sixth days'. Samuelson also produces a delightful insight into what appears to be contradictions by the Jewish commentators but are in fact not contradictions at all. He takes as his analogy the denary and binary systems in Base Mathematics and notes that, although there are two answers, both are correct. Therefore, what appears as a contradiction is not a contradiction at all, as it is dealing with two different premises. Samuelson defines Jewish commentators who have apparently different opinions as those who share the same truth with their 'epistemological unity having diverse expressions'. In his analysis of the Jewish commentators, Samuelson unearths some beautiful gems. Commentating on '*Vayomer Elokim yehi raqia*' (Genesis 1:6) - Rashi links the creation of the world with the power of speech, as the firmament's creation - was preceded by 'And G-d said'. Just as G-d's power of speech created the universe, so the power of speech is filtered down to man so that he can create peace and harmony. Another of Samuelson's gems is concerned with G-d's consideration for the feelings of his Angels which is stressed by Rashi and the Midrashic commentators, because of the phrase 'Na'aseh Adam' (Genesis 1:26), which is in the collective imperative: 'G-d sought the consent of his Angels because in making humans He gave them certain powers that would otherwise fall within the authority of the angels'.

For Samuelson the Judaic and latter-Greek interpretation of the Creation is that the structure of the universe is subservient to the pattern of the universe, and therefore atoms do not create forces but forces create atoms. Plato's masterpiece *Timaeus* was a response to the pre-Socratic philosophers who wished to see creation as a purely mechanical concept based on 'a single kind of substance which became a different element, depending on the state of the primary material'. It is ironic that these early Greek philosophers see eye-to-eye with modern scientists and physical philosophers who try to reduce all creation to an atomic structure: 'The reigning voices of Greek scientists were in fact modem day atomists in the sense that they maintained that everything in the universe is reducible to particles of the same nature that combine and separate from each other'. Plato's

Timaeus sought to prove that the opposite was the case. All acts of creation were 'the results of the Deity's persuasion of the Creation'. The Creation contains three elements, the first of which is *reason* which is its blueprint. *Necessity*, the second element, is the physical manifestation of the blueprint and *chance*, the third element is the inter–elemental activity which caused evolution. Chance is only how it appears to the subjective mind and is, therefore, a totally structured part of the creation thus giving another Kantian example of the phenomenic basis of chance being different to the noumena basis of chance. Creation is, therefore, 'a picture of a Deity eternally using reason to persuade purposeless, natural chaos to a reasonable, purposeful, moral order'. The link between the Greek and Jewish version of the Creation is summed up beautifully by Samuelson: 'the *ought* determines the quality of the *is*'. Objects either regress to their origin or progress towards G–d and therefore the creation of the world 'is to be understood in terms of ethics'. For Samuelson, progress would therefore be defined as the ability of the object of G–d's creation to escape from the evil force in the world to return totally to its creator. It could therefore be summed up that the principal of this book is that of 'imitato D–i' which 'is to do what moves the Created Universe in the direction of its redemption'.

Peter Ochs of Drew University describes the book as 'highbrow' and to an extent, Samuelson reverts to an ivory tower and imagines that he's lecturing to PhD physics students, but on the whole the book is excellent and well written, with its 'highbrowness' often lifting the reader to a better understanding of the physical attributes of the universe.

Samuelson interprets the verse from Leviticus 9:2, 'You shall be holy because I, the Lord your G–d am holy' as the fact that G–d had to divide that which was unified — His essence, into that which is separated, which is His Creation and that our role as His created ones is to separate ourselves from the negative forces of regression and attach ourselves to the positive forces of redemption. This is the principle of Samuelson's book and this is why its title is so apt.

On Ageing

By Jean Amery
Bloomington, Indiana: University Press, 1994
[ISBN 0 2533 0675 2 £17.50 132p]

The power of this book reaches the inner self because the contents of this book apply to each of us individually and because it hits upon many truths. Whoever reads this book must be affected by it because what this book contains affects us all.

The subject of *On Ageing* may best be termed 'social time', not time that actually is, but time that is perceived. An example Jean Amery gives of social time is the perception of a boring period of one's life followed by an intense, exciting, period of one's life: 'For person A, the years 1939–45 are opaque and heavy... the ten years preceding the war experience have become lifeless and slight in his memory ... these six years are longer, weightier time than the previous ten'. Thus, objectively, the ten years before the war are longer than the six years of the war but subjectively the six years of the war are much longer.

From social perception of time Amery leads on to social perception of ageing and from that, to the social perception of death. The depth with which Amery examines all these issues is painfully deep and is consequently full of fascinating insights. One such insight is that it is impossible to use the verb 'die' in the present tense as 'dying only gets its logical justification through the entrance of death'. The result of dying must therefore refer back to the past.

The problem of this book is not whether Amery is accurate in his observations of people's reaction to time, ageing, illness and death but whether morally, such deep introspection is necessary. Amery's example of the woman who examines herself in the mirror every morning since discovering nodules on her face may be full of accurate observations but does not question the fact, that she is there in the first place. This lady 'fifty years old practices in front of her mirror a business of self-assessment... even a resistance to the ego flecked with yellow and looking back at her from the mirror'. If this lady had lived a worthwhile life, would this ritual have been undergone in the first place? One would not think very well of a Chassidic Rebbetzen engaged in this activity because one would feel that the nearer one got to G-d, the less one is likely to worry about such things. Amery is taking his approach to the 'ravages of time' from a secular angle and all his characters are members of the secular public. His trendy oldster who 'carries himself young and fashionably, marries a young woman and while wheezing does the jerk at sixty' is more likely to be found at an Anglo-Jewish wedding than an ultra-Orthodox wedding. The book is devastatingly accurate but only to those whose lives are secularly based.

The devastating accuracy of the book is reflected in its social observations. The trendy oldster is explained by his reaction to the media around him: 'Those who remain young in splendour do not find themselves in agreement with society but no doubt in accord with its economic and publicistic facade'. The supreme irony is that the same society that exhorts them to be young, practices ageism when they apply for jobs: 'The heads of personnel... won't employ a beginner at the age of forty and Mr X who from twenty-three to forty has computed foreign-exchange notes will do the same for two and a half decades or more'. When one reaches a certain age society makes a judgement and 'as scrap-iron of the mind we belong to the waste-heaps of the epoch'.

Amery defines death as 'a virus we have when we enter the world' and as we grow older it 'comes out of its latency' and overwhelms our thoughts and actions. This secular perception of death lead to an even more bizarre destiny. Amery's autobiographical A, fears death after the ageing process, more than death from external means. Amery, as a survivor of Auschwitz, includes even external death from the epitome of evil on Earth as not as bad as death from ageing. The type of death where 'a boot would have kicked me to pieces or half kicked me to pieces and where nobody would have given my mashed body a glance' would still have been more preferable to Amery then death by ageing. The fact that 'as ageing people we become alien to our bodies and at the same time closer to their sluggish mass' was worse for Amery than those 'who had been strung up on powerful iron hooks' in

Auschwitz, is a powerful indictment to those who see death in secular terms.

The fascinating and profound insights of Amery's sociological observations are perceived in the final days before dying: 'The rich man passes on in a luxury clinic with flowers on his table, the well honoured, personally tinted care of the doctors and the visit of dependants that can happen every hour whereas the poor man ends up in a home for the ageing, in hospital or in a badly heated apartment where the mortally ill have to drag themselves to the corridor to go to the toilet. Amery then quotes the Yiddish proverb '*Iz men hot gelt, krechsen men* – it is easier to cry with money'.

Jean Amery was born as Hans Meyer in Vienna of a Jewish father. Amery is an anagram of Meyer. Maybe, if Amery had reassembled the letters back to Meyer again and embraced some of the Judaic tenets concerning life, death, ageing, illness and time, the tragic suicide of a man so gifted in thought and language would have been avoided.

Evil and Suffering in Jewish Philosophy

By Oliver Leaman
Cambridge: Cambridge University Press, 1995
[ISBN No: 0521 417 244 257p]

The achievement of this profoundly brilliant book is Oliver Leaman's ability to simplify the complicated, to clarify the obscure and to unravel the complex. The complexity of Spinoza's Conatus, an internal absorber of how events in life affect us, is unravelled by Leaman as a 'system of ideas and images which the individual acquires through his contact with his causal history both internal and external'. The complication of Mendlessohn's Judaism in trying to synthesise Germanic culture and Judaism is summed up by Leaman 'if only the Germans knew what Judaism was all about they would appreciate that it forms an acceptable basis to life as a German citizen and if only the Jews knew what civil society was all about they would appreciate that it is an acceptable context within which to live a Jewish life'. What would Mendlessohn have made of events one and a half centuries later when the Germans' knowledge of Judaism was used to exacerbate the suffering of the Jewish people even further, as when food suddenly became available to concentration camp inmates on Yom Kippur? The obscurity of Herman Cohen's Kantian moral imperatives in relation to his Judaic socialism is clarified by Leaman as 'treating the interests of others on a par with one's own interests and acting in line with universally rational principles'.

The theme of this book is how philosophers from Philo to Fackenheim have tried to incorporate evil into good. What is interesting is that none of the philosophers quoted have formulated the idea that as good by its definition must be totally free of evil, evil exists totally separately from good. Gershonides touches on this idea by implying that if G-d had created the Earth with total goodness and evil had appeared *after* the Creation, then 'nothing can be done once the Organisation is set up' and that evil has to be fought with the processes of Creation, namely the Torah. If, however, one wishes to incorporate evil into good, then one has to argue that evil as we know it, is not evil at all. Leaman's brilliance in discussing the philosophical analysis of evil is in using the Book of Job as his yardstick. Evil, as we know it, inflicted itself on Job and Job's reaction to it, plus the reaction of his comforters is very fertile ground on which to plant the philosophical analysis of evil. Fackenheim would argue that events of the Holocaust superseded themselves over the Book of Job and that therefore the Book of Job cannot be used as a yardstick. However, Leaman does not accept this view and maintains that 'many instances of slaughter of innocent Jews preceded the Holocaust' and that therefore the Holocaust itself does not alter an analysis of evil based on the Book of Job.

Leaman introduces the Book of Job by devoting a chapter to it and attempts to glean from it certain premises to be used in later chapters in his philosophical analysis of evil. One interesting observation from which Leaman drew a premise is that all three of Job's comforters, Eliphaz, Bildad and Zophar, were rebuked by G–d, whereas Job's fortunes were eventually restored in abundance. The implication of this is that G–d respects dialogue from his Created Ones more than mere submissiveness and that man's relationship with G–d 'is not based on a simple reward–and–punishment level but lies much deeper than that'. Evil exists in the world and G–d actually rebukes those who submissively accept it without question.

As Sa'adiah Gaon actually wrote a commentary on the Book of Job it is easy to ascertain how Sa'adiah analyses evil from its texts. The pain that all life–forms receive in this world is recompensed in the world–to–come. It may be that we 'dislike being obliged to move on to a different form even if it be to our advantage,' but the fact that it is to our advantage means that pain or early death are not in themselves evil if they are replaced by something better. Leaman's profound knowledge of Arabic philosophy enables him to place Sa'adiah amongst the Mutazalite thinkers of his time who believed that G–d's revelation is perceived from good as against the Asherites who believed that good is perceived from G–d's revelation 'For Sa'adiah and the Mutazalites G–d does what is just because it is just.'

In the case of Moses Mendlessohn, the Book of Job is particularly apt. After losing a child at eleven months he writes 'my innocent child didn't die in vain... her mind made outstanding progress in that period ... One could see the blossoming of the passion like the sprouting of young grass when it pierces the hard crust of Earth in Spring'. But for Mendlessohn, who took the Leibnizian view that this is the best possible of all possible worlds, this is not a tragedy because the world would not regulate itself in the way it has without these tragedies. The lion could not live without the zebra. This view of Mendlessohn would totally explain G–d's admonition of Job who 'describes at length the extreme effort He has made in order to organise the world efficiently'. For Mendlessohn G–d is admonishing Job to make him realise that for the world to be what it is all events have to occur to make it what it is.

The Book of Job is also used by Leaman to highlight the philosophical differences between Gershonides and Maimonides. For Maimonides evil is linked to matter and thus to nature and it is, therefore, illogical to express only observations about G–d based on nature and matter: 'G–d's connection with such contingent phenomena is bound to be very distant since G–d is a necessary being and, as such, completely independent of such phenomena'. However, Gershonides, like Rabbi Abraham Isaac Kook, regarded nature as reflecting G–d's genius and justice and was therefore 'quite happy to look at the ways in which the world is structured for clues as to the intentions and capacity of G–d'. If Job were to have adopted Maimonides' approach he would merely have highlighted the huge difference between himself and G–d, so that there is no link between man's knowledge and G–d's knowledge 'except the Word itself'. If Job were to adopt Gershonides' approach he would unite reason and intellect and the apparent evil in nature would be understood and this 'would enable him to make free decisions and find an escape route' from evil.

However, all diagnosis of evil based on the Book of Job will come to nought if we accept the views of post–Holocaust philosophers, such as Fackenheim, Rubinstein and Arthur Cohen, that the Holocaust was unique, as in Fackenheim's words 'a *novum*' or in Cohen's words 'a tremendum'. If Auschwitz puts flesh on the bones of evil, then it is harder to theorise on evil just as a concept. It is hardly possible to tell a concentration camp survivor of the Maimonidian concept of the enormous gulf between G–d and man, and that he is guilty of an inappropriate conception of the deity' if he hoped for G–d's intervention in the survival of himself and his family. It would perhaps give more compensation to the concentration camp survivors to unite the Gershonidian concept of reason and intellect and this would therefore make the Gershonidian analysis of evil more relevant to the Holocaust. If the evil of the Holocaust is unique then because it is unique, it must not triumph. Therefore, for Fackenheim, post-Holocaust Jewry must rise above the evil and touch the Ultimate, rekindling man's relationship with G-d and obeying the six-hundred-and-fourteenth commandment 'that the Jewish people should not offer Hitler any posthumous victory by disappearing through the throwing off of their faith'. The action of the Nazis to turn G-d's 'instruction-book' upside-down is responsible for the uniqueness of the Holocaust, according to Arthur Cohen: 'During the Holocaust a certain segment of humanity behaved immorally and without reference to the rules of behaviour which are available to everyone and G-d cannot be blamed for it'. These were the perpetrators of Cohen's tremendum and of whom Judaism would call Amalek. Rubinstein's concept of the uniqueness of the evil of the Holocaust leads him to abandon G-d completely but to still continue the rituals of Judaism 'as they still love a rôle to play in their powerful psychological symbolism'. Besides breaking Fackenheim's six-hundred-and-fourteenth commandment, he has reduced psychological symbolism to nothingness since a symbol has to refer to something to be called a symbol: a Shofar that does not symbolise a return to G-d's ways becomes a ram's horn.

Another of Leaman's attributes is to bring a helpful psychological analysis of how evil affects the human condition. Spinoza's concept of absorbing events into our internal natures 'which are all different and unique' would apply particularly to Holocaust survivors whose conatus would be enlarged to accommodate the terrible events that they had witnessed. It must be remembered that the Spinozan conatus is enlarged both when the survivor witnesses evil acts done to others as well as evil acts done to himself. An example of this would be a son witnessing gold coins being yanked out of his father's mouth without anaesthetic. Maimonides' profound notion that evil is caused by an excessive appetite 'which we quite readily impose upon ourselves through our greedy and inappropriate attitude to the world and its resources' is applicable to the addicted victims of over-affluence. Martin Buber's observation of the *I – it* relationship, when the 'it' part of the relationship is based solely on the needs of the 'I', is a warning to people who 'treat others as means to an end, generally *their* ends'.

Finally, it must be stated that the quality of his writing of his own ideas is equal to the quality of his writing of others' ideas. Leaman makes the brilliant assertion that the Holocaust couldn't be construed in any way as a punishment as it was more likely that less decent people would escape the evil snare of the Nazis because they would be 'usually more successful in escaping suffering than their more gullible and virtuous peers'. Leaman's book may not help us to escape from evil but it may enable us to understand it better.

Index